Asthma

For Jackie and Katy   F. C.

Text copyright © 1982, 1999 Althea Braithwaite
Illustrations copyright © 1999 Frances Cony

The moral rights of the author and of the illustrator
have been asserted.

This edition first published 1999 by Happy Cat Books,
Bradfield, Essex CO11 2UT

A CIP catalogue record for this book is available from
the British Library

ISBN 1 899248 38 2 Paperback
ISBN 1 899248 33 1 Hardback

Printed in Hong Kong by Wing King Tong Co. Ltd

1899 248 331 4901

618.92238

TALKING IT THROUGH

Asthma

Althea

Illustrated by Frances Cony

Happy Cat Books

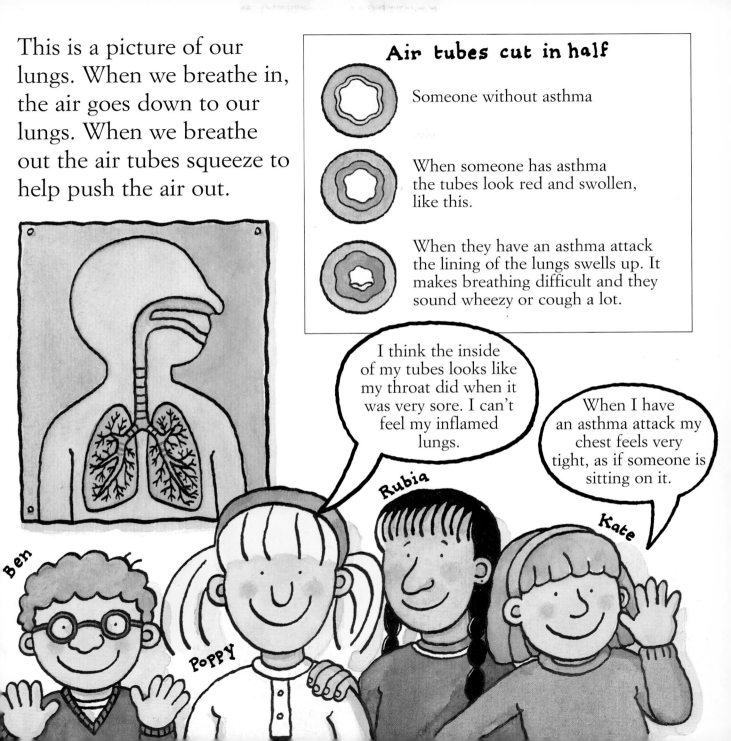

Most of the time we can avoid asthma attacks. Many people take medicine each night and morning. We call these medicines *Preventers* because they prevent us from having an asthma attack.

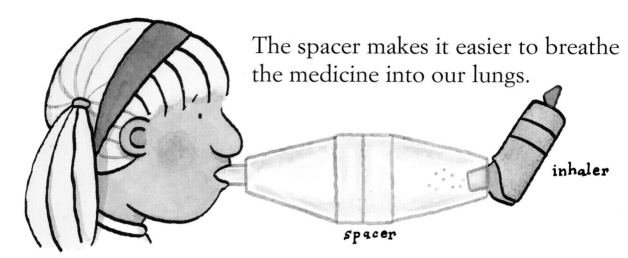

The spacer makes it easier to breathe the medicine into our lungs.

inhaler

spacer

People with asthma have one of these blue inhalers which they carry around with them. If they get wheezy, or if they know they might get wheezy, they take a puff. We call these medicines *Relievers* because they make it easier to breathe.

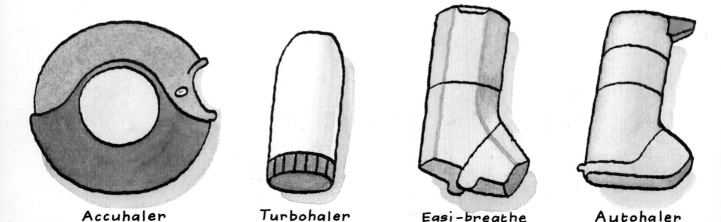

Accuhaler   Turbohaler   Easi-breathe   Autohaler

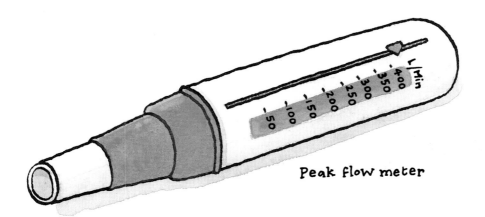

Peak flow meter

This shows how hard I can blow out. Sometimes, the reading is lower than usual and I am wheezy or coughing. I need to take extra preventer and reliever until I am better.

You must never take other people's medicines.

Rotahaler   Diskhaler

Rubia showed the assembly her blue inhaler. She called it a reliever. "I don't get asthma badly, so I just carry this about with me, and if I start to get wheezy I take a puff."

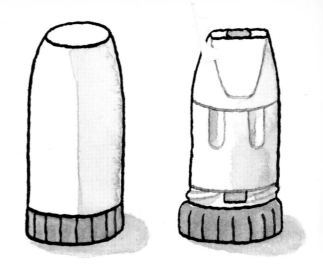

The excitement of getting the display together and standing up in front of all the children made her a bit wheezy. She got her inhaler out and showed the children how she used it.

"I breathe out, then put the inhaler between my lips and breathe in deeply. I hold my breath to let the medicine into my lungs, then slowly breathe out."

Ben said that most of the time people wouldn't know he has asthma. He takes his preventative medicine night and morning to stop asthma affecting him.

He brought a used up inhaler and his spacer into school, so he could demonstrate what he has to do. He shook the inhaler and then attached it to the clear plastic bubble.

"I put the spacer in my mouth, press the inhaler and breathe in the medicine. It goes down into my air tubes to stop them from getting swollen."

"After taking it, I clean my teeth and rinse my mouth, just in case any of the medicine has gone into my mouth."

Ben has to remember to take his medicine every day to keep him fit and well. If he starts to get a cold he takes extra medicine and this usually stops him from having an asthma attack.

Kate has brought in her peak flow meter to show the children.

She blows into it each night and morning before taking her medicine. It shows how well her lungs are working. Her mum then knows how much medicine she should take.

"I hold the meter like this, then I take a deep breath and blow hard. I try three blows and then mark my best score on a graph. I take my graph to show the asthma nurse at the clinic."

"This is my graph."

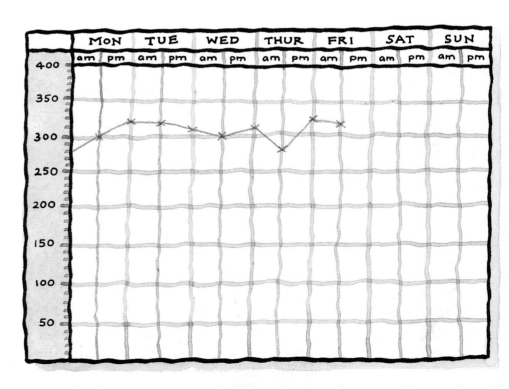

dust mite
[enlarged]

Poppy tells the children that she goes to the asthma clinic at the health centre. "I go three or four times a year. The asthma nurse knows me well! She measures me and weighs me to make sure I am growing properly. She showed me the chart. It looks as though I'll be taller than mum when I finish growing."

"I show her that I remember how to use my inhaler. Sometimes I'm getting it a bit wrong and she puts me right again. When I'm older I may change to a different inhaler, and not need my spacer. We talk about my medicines. I tell them which ones my friends have and which one I like the most."

eight

Joe says he doesn't just have asthma. He has eczema too. "When it's bad the skin behind my ears and knees gets very red and sore. I have to try not to scratch it." Not only that, but he gets hayfever in the summer. "On bad days I have a runny nose and swollen eyes. People think I've got a cold." He thinks life is very unfair. "I need extra creams and medicines to help those," he says.

His dad has hayfever, and he had asthma and eczema when he was young. Joe hopes he will grow out of them too.

Janek said that his teddies have to spend a night in the freezer each week! "It's to kill the house dust mites." They go in on different nights, so he always has one to cuddle up to. His toy rabbit gets washed weekly with his sheets.

He tells them that his asthma is caused by house dust mites and probably pets. To make it easier to keep his room clean dad has taken up the carpet and put down lino. "It's much better for my cars. Our cats have to live outside now that I have asthma."

Ben tells them about learning he had asthma. "I used to get lots of chesty colds. One bad winter mum said I was very wheezy and coughing all the time. The doctor thought it was asthma and she gave me medicine. She wanted me to go the hospital to be seen by the specialist doctor and nurse in the chest clinic."

"The nurse asked me to blow into a machine to see if my lungs were working properly. I had to take a deep breath and then blow hard into a tube. She showed me the numbers on the machine and said she thought I could do better. I took a deep breath and blew really hard. She was really pleased with me, and she pressed a button to print out the results."

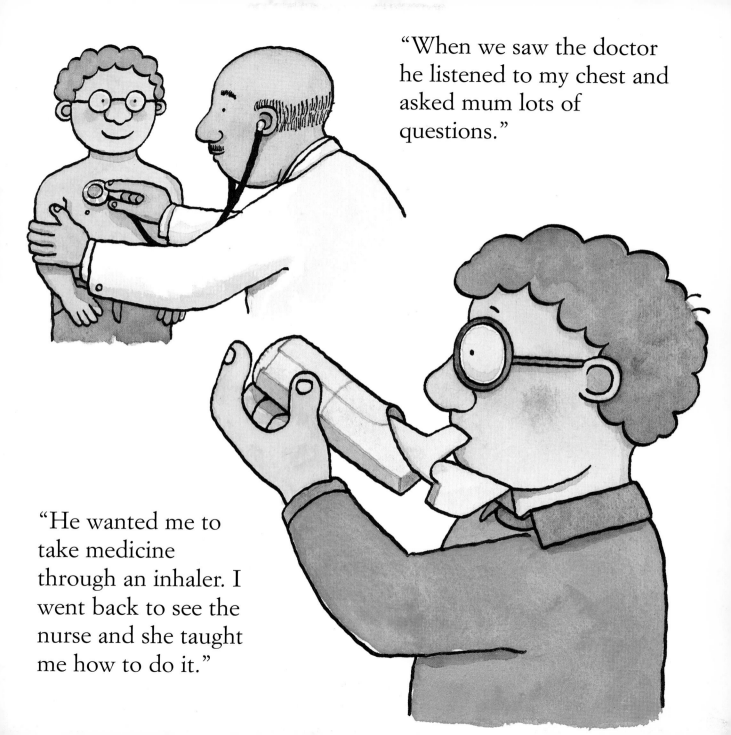

"When we saw the doctor he listened to my chest and asked mum lots of questions."

"He wanted me to take medicine through an inhaler. I went back to see the nurse and she taught me how to do it."

Before the doctors had worked out how much medicine she needed, Kate sometimes got very ill. She would keep herself and her family awake with her coughing. Sometimes she had a bad asthma attack in the night. Mum or dad would come and give her extra medicine and comfort her until she felt better.

One night she had a really bad attack and the medicine didn't work. "I felt very frightened and panicky. Mum sat with me while dad phoned the doctor. I think they were worried too. The doctor came and gave me pills and extra reliever which made me better very quickly."

He was very kind. He gave mum some pills for me to take over the next few days.

Roy has a bit of a cold and at lunchtime it gives him an asthma attack. He starts coughing and wheezing and he finds it difficult to get his breath. His friends help him to find his blue inhaler. The dinner ladies are very worried. Roy wishes he could tell them that he's all right.

After about five minutes the medicine starts to work and Roy feels better. The dinner lady gives him a glass of water. Later the children ask if the dinner ladies would like to see their asthma display.

Poppy tells them that no one can decide what causes her asthma. "When I went to the clinic they did some scratch tests to try and find out. They put some drops of special liquid on my arm and scratched each one with a needle. It didn't hurt but later it was a bit itchy."

"We don't have a dog or cat at home because they think that might make my asthma worse. I sometimes play with my friend's dog and it doesn't always make me wheeze."

Janek says that grass pollen affects him as well as dust mites. He always takes a couple of puffs from his inhaler before he goes on a picnic. He keeps his inhaler in his pocket just in case he needs it later. Mum warns him not to roll in the grass. "As if I would!"

"Mum got very worried when I was going camping last week. She thought I might forget to take my medicine. I took my record card with me and marked it off."

"I wouldn't have forgotten anyway because I always take it before cleaning my teeth."

Kate says that some Olympic champions have asthma. "I didn't think I would ever be good at games. Running about always made me cough and get short of breath. My chest hurts too. Now I use my inhaler before we do PE or play games outside. It stops my asthma coming on. I sometimes use my inhaler when I am in the middle of playing games too."

"Sometimes when it's very cold I don't go cross-country running. My friend Sally goes, she is a very fast runner even though she's got asthma."

Like adults, children find it easier to treat their illnesses if they understand what is going on.

The incidence of asthma seems to be rising, and around one in six young children have recurrent episodes of cough or wheeze, especially with viral infections. Most of these children improve as they grow, but others keep having symptoms and require regular treatment. New treatments and delivery systems have vastly improved our ability to control symptoms in children and it is now very unusual for children to be so affected by their disease that it limits their activities in a major way.

Althea's book, recently rewritten to reflect the changes in asthma care, explains to these children and to those around them "What is asthma?" and shows some of the ways of dealing with it. This understanding is particularly important because much of the treatment is nowadays in the hands of the child as well as the parents, teachers and doctors.

Dr Rob Ross Russell

Consultant Paediatrician
Addenbrooke's Hospital, Cambridge